S0-ABC-902

KID'S
TRIP
DIARY

MARLOR PRESS
BOOKS FOR KIDS

Kid's Squish Book
Slimy, squishy, sticky things to do that should only be done
wearing your oldest clothes

Kid's Book to Welcome a New Baby
A fun activity book of things to do and to learn
for "big sister" or "big brother"

My Camp Book
Campers! Write up your own adventures
and experiences

Kid's Trip Diary
A fun diary and vacation book to use while traveling.
Many happy hours ahead.

Also

Tale of a Cat
A journal you can keep about
the life and times of your feline friend

Kid's Trip Diary

Kid's! Write up your own
adventures and experiences.
Have fun for hours!

MARLOR PRESS

SAINT PAUL, MINNESOTA

KID'S
TRIP
DIARY

Revised edition
Copyright 1998 by Marlin and Loris Bree

KID'S TRIP DIARY. Published by Marlor Press, Inc. All rights reserved,
including all under International and Pan American Copyright conventions.
No part of this book may be reproduced in any form or by any means,
electronic or mechanical, including photocopy, recording or any
storage and retrieval system now known or to be invented,
without the written permission of the publisher, except by a reviewer
who wishes to quote brief passages in connection with a review
written for inclusion in a magazine, newspaper, or broadcast.

Special thanks to all the kids, educators, parents & others
who contributed to this book, especially Bernice Gutzmer

ISBN 0-943400-98-8

Copyright 1988, 1990, 1992, 1995
and 1998 by Marlin and Loris Bree.

Disclaimer: This book does not endorse any particular product,
supplier, or service. Examples and games presented
are for the purpose of general entertainment and information only.
Marlor Press and the authors are not responsible for any loss,
inconvenience, injury or property damage of any kind.
Not responsible for errors and omissions.

MARLOR PRESS, INC.
4304 Brigadoon Drive
Saint Paul, Minnesota   55126

CONTENTS

HOW TO HAVE FUN WITH THIS BOOK

Congratulations! You're going on a trip.

This book can help make your vacation a lot more fun. You can write about your own travel adventures and discoveries. It will be your friend for many happy travel hours.

Your **KID'S TRIP DIARY** is divided into three parts:

1/ Getting ready   2/ On the Road   3/ Memories

1/ **Getting ready** helps you get ready for your trip. You can make plans for what you want to see and do. It's fun to think about your vacation.

2/ **On the road** is for when you travel. You write about your adventures. You tell what you did, what you liked best, and what you saw. Play a new game every day. Wow, some vacation!

3/ **Memories**. All good vacations come to an end, but you will have a souvenir after your trip is over. Paste in a ticket to a fun park, a picture you took, or a postcard you bought. Save your best memories of your trip and your people. Pick out your favorite places and events as you look back through your book.

A SPECIAL NOTE TO PARENTS

This book will make traveling more fun for a child. It will also make it easier for him or her to travel with the family.

When a child takes a part in preparing for a vacation or trip, he or she makes an investment in the journey. A child can look forward to travel as fun and adventure.

Help your child get information about where you are going. You can do this on the Internet or get a book or a magazine. You can help your child write a letter to a local chamber of commerce or state tourism board (your local library has addresses). It will be exciting to have a packet of information come addressed to your child.

Help your child make a short list of what he or she wants to see and do on the trip. This lets the child anticipate the trip as a fun adventure.

Help your child prepare for the trip. Perhaps a pet needs to be boarded. Or a plant or garden needs caring for by a friend. Write these things down, and, when they are done, the child can check them.

Children should help decide what to take along on the trip. They can help pack their own bags of clothing and supplies. You can also help the child fill out information to take along, such as *Who I want to send cards to.* You can make this a positive experience by your attitude and your words.

Travel is fun if there's lots to do. Take along favorite toys and games.

You can also go over the *Today's Diary* pages, helping them capture some of their trip in writing. Children will be encouraged by making writing fun.

Keep in mind that they will be quickly discouraged by criticism or even the suggestion that what they've done could be improved. If your child is too small to write, just ask the child to tell you what he or she wants to say. Remember to write the same short, simple sentences that your child uses. You don't have to be fancy, but your child will remember your love and your interest.

Children enjoy having a little allowance of their own. On the diary pages, they can record what they spent and their daily totals. This teaches money management and can help make the vacation special.

It's important to be very supportive of children during travel. Give them your attention and encouragement. Tell them when you think that what they have done is wonderful. Always be positive and soon you will see gradual improvement in their communication abilities.

Relax and let your child have fun with this book. You will both have a better time on vacation.

A checklist of fun things to take

- A game bag, filled with different play things. Your child can draw a new one each day.
- Washable markers and colored pencils to draw in the *Kid's Trip Diary.*
- Maps of the trip with your route marked. Your child can also mark places you stop.
- Spending money for your child to carry and use. (Be sure to have your child mark this down in the Daily Diary's *What I bought today.*)
- Small pillow to make your child comfortable.
- Healthy snacks and healthy drinks, avoiding sugar (Keep these in a cooler if you are traveling by automobile or van.)
- A portable cassette or CD player, along with the child's favorite music or spoken books. (Perhaps a new one might be purchased for the trip — or borrowed from the library.)
- Magazines and books. (Some old favorites, plus some from the library.)
- Some extra writing supplies, such as a large paper tablet.
- A small cardboard box for special travel souvenirs, such as picture postcards, small souvenirs or tickets to parks or rides (you can paste the best of these in the last section of this book to make it a permanent record.)
- Pack several favorite books for reading aloud.

PART ONE

GETTING READY

STEPS TO GET READY
WHAT I TO DO BEFORE I GO
WHAT I WANT TO SEE AND DO
WHAT I WANT TO TAKE ALONG
IMPORTANT TO TAKE ALONG
WHO I WANT TO SEND CARDS TO
I DON'T WANT TO FORGET

STEPS TO GET READY

You can have as much fun getting ready as really traveling. That's because there's a lot to think about and learn.

Here are five things to do before you go:

1. You'll want to **get ready.** The first thing is to think about what you need to do before you go. Do you have a pet that needs someone to take care of it? A plant that needs watering? Write that down.

2. Learn about **where you are going**. You can visit the Internet (An adult can help). You can use books or magazines at the library and you can write to the state or city you plan to visit. Libraries have all kinds of addresses. Write down what **you want to see and do**. Talk about it with the adults traveling with you.

3. Think about toys, games and clothes **to take with you.** List the things you want to take. Remember it is much easier to pack toys that are little.

4. Write down **information to take along**. This means family names and emergency telephone numbers.

5. Think of how pleased a friend, a grandparent, or an aunt will be when they get a note from you. Write down the names and addresses of people you want **to send cards to**.

Travel is fun. Find out about your trip. Talk about some things you'd like to do. Help make plans and be willing to do what others want to do. Pack some of your own things. Enjoy yourself. Have a great time.

1. WHAT I WANT TO DO BEFORE I GO

1/ _____

2/ _____

3/ _____

4/ _____

5/ _____

6/ _____

7/ _____

8/ _____

9/ _____

10/ _____

11/ _____

12/ _____

13/ _____

14/ _____

2. WHAT I WANT TO SEE AND DO ON MY TRIP

1/ _____

2/ _____

3/ _____

4/ _____

5/ _____

6/ _____

7/ _____

8/ _____

9/ _____

10/ _____

11/ _____

12/ _____

13 _____

14 _____

3. WHAT I WANT TO TAKE ALONG

1/ _____

2/ _____

3/ _____

4/ _____

5/ _____

6/ _____

7/ _____

8/ _____

9/ _____

10/ _____

11/ _____

12 _____

13/ _____

14/ _____

4. IMPORTANT TO TAKE ALONG

MY NAME

My home address

City   State   Zip or postal code

My Telephone: Area code (   )

Height   Weight   Age

The name of the adult I am with and where we will stay

In case of emergency, please contact at home

Name:

Telephone: (Area Code   )

My doctor or clinic:

Telephone: (Area Code   )

My special medical needs:

Special instructions in case of emergency

5. WHO I WANT TO SEND CARDS TO

Name

Address

City   State   Zip or postal code

Name

Address

City   State   Zip or postal code

Name

Address

City   State   Zip or postal code

Name

Address

City   State   Zip or postal code

I DON'T WANT
TO FORGET

Perhaps you will want to remind yourself to pack a special game or a special toy. Or, when you get to your vacation place, to send notes home to friends.

_____

_____

_____

_____

_____

_____

_____

_____

_____

_____

_____

PART TWO

ON THE ROAD

HOW TO USE
YOUR DAILY DIARY

YOUR TRAVEL DIARY

EXTRA GAMES TO PLAY

PUZZLES

☆ HOW TO USE YOUR DAILY DIARY

You can jot something down for every day of your trip. It's fun and it helps you keep a wonderful record.

Each day of your trip is told in **Today's Diary**. There are **two pages** for every day of your trip. There are enough pages for 28 days.

If you go on a shorter trip, you can use **more pages** when you have a lot to tell.

There is a new **game** for each day of your trip and some extra games in the back of the book.

At the top

Here you write the date, what the weather is like, and where you are. You don't have to be fancy about the weather, just say something like "sunny" or "it rained all day". Talk to your adults about where you are.

22

TODAY'S

DATE: *July 7, 1999* OUR WEATHER IS: *Sunny!*
TODAY WE ARE IN: *Orlando, Florida*

What we did today

This is your place to write down some of the things you did today. Here you can list what you did, even if it wasn't your favorite.

What we did today: *We spent the day at Disneyland. What fun!*

Things I liked best

Think of what was the most fun or interested you the most. Write that down.

Things I liked best: *The haunted house. Loved the rides.*

What I saw or heard today that was funny

Perhaps something funny happened to you or someone with you. Or you saw something that you felt good about. Write it down.

What I saw or heard that was funny: *The spooks in the haunted house.*

Some foods I ate

Here you can tell some of the favorite things you ate or drank today.
Be certain to tell if you tried anything new and you really liked it.

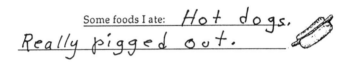

Some foods I ate: *Hot dogs.*
Really pigged out.

Did you buy anything today?

You may have a little travel money of your own to spend and to
record. Write down what you bought today. This could be something to
eat, something to keep or a present for someone else.

WHAT I BOUGHT TODAY

ITEM	COST
Mousketeer hat	$ *8.95*
D. Duck T shirt	$ *12.95*
	$
	$
TOTAL I SPENT TODAY:	$ *21.90*

At the end of the day, add up what you spend. Then count how much
you have left. Do you have to make your money last for the whole trip?
Maybe you will want to put it in a pile for each day left. Then you'll
know how much you have to spend.

Draw something you saw today

Draw a picture of something you liked today. Below it, write a few words explaining a little about your picture. It will be fun to look back at what you drew at the end of the trip.

My picture is about: _M. Mouse with Mom and me!_

Now, go on and start your trip. We hope you have a lot of fun.

TODAY'S

DATE: _____   OUR WEATHER IS: _____

TODAY WE ARE IN: _____

What we did today: _____

_____

_____

_____

Things I liked best: _____

_____

_____

What I saw or heard that was funny: _____

_____

_____

Some foods I ate: _____

_____

WHAT I BOUGHT TODAY

ITEM   COST

_____ $_____

_____ $_____

_____ $_____

_____ $_____

TOTAL I SPENT TODAY: $_____

DIARY

DRAW SOMETHING YOU SAW TODAY

My picture is about: _____

_____

THE TEMPLE OF DOOM

The **Temple of Doom** lies somewhere ahead. You will get caught in the Temple if you say the **Forbidden Word,** which you agree on in advance. It can be any ordinary word, in fact, the more ordinary the better. That's so you can trip up your players and send them to the **Temple of Doom**, where they have to remain silent for the next 5 miles or 5 minutes. Good words *not* to be spoken are "yes," "no," or perhaps, (toughest of all), "I." You can start a conversation about anything, but the person who says the **Forbidden Word** is banished to the **Temple of Doom.** To vary the game, you can have several **Forbidden Words.**

TODAY'S

DATE: _____ OUR WEATHER IS: _____

TODAY WE ARE IN: _____

What we did today: _____

_____

_____

_____

Things I liked best: _____

_____

_____

What I saw or heard that was funny: _____

_____

_____

Some foods I ate: _____

_____

WHAT I BOUGHT TODAY

ITEM	COST
_____	$_____
_____	$_____
_____	$_____
_____	$_____

TOTAL I SPENT TODAY: $_____

DIARY

DRAW SOMETHING YOU SAW TODAY

My picture is about:

 TRUE COLORS

Pick a **favorite color** and look for objects that are this color. For example, as you drive down the highway, you can say, "I see a red barn." Or, "I see a red car." The object is to see who can get the most objects of the **chosen color** in 15 minutes. Each player in turn can choose a **different color.** After you play this game for a while, you can make it a little harder by saying what you will or will not count. For example, you could count only objects of a chosen color—which are not cars. Or trucks.

TODAY'S

DATE: _____   OUR WEATHER IS: _____

TODAY WE ARE IN: _____

What we did today: _____
_____
_____
_____

Things I liked best: _____
_____
_____

What I saw or heard that was funny: _____
_____
_____

Some foods I ate: _____
_____

WHAT I BOUGHT TODAY

ITEM   COST

_____ $_____

_____ $_____

_____ $_____

_____ $_____

TOTAL I SPENT TODAY: $_____

DIARY

DRAW SOMETHING YOU SAW TODAY

My picture is about: _____

_____

_____

I SEE

The first player **looks about**, perhaps out of the window of the car, then gives **one clue**, such as, *"I see something red."* The others have to **guess** what he or she sees. Each has one guess. The winner gets to be in charge of the next round of **"I see."**

TODAY'S

DATE: _____   OUR WEATHER IS: _____

TODAY WE ARE IN: _____

What we did today: _____

_____

_____

_____

Things I liked best: _____

_____

_____

What I saw or heard that was funny: _____

_____

_____

Some foods I ate: _____

_____

WHAT I BOUGHT TODAY

ITEM   COST

_____ $_____

_____ $_____

_____ $_____

_____ $_____

TOTAL I SPENT TODAY: $_____

DIARY

DRAW SOMETHING YOU SAW TODAY

My picture is about: _____

_____

I PACKED MY BAG (WOW!)

You've probably never **packed a bag** like this before where you are limited only by your **imagination**. Name an object to pack, then say, *"I packed my bag, and in it I have a tank* (or whatever you decide). Then the next player says, *"I packed my bag and in it I have a tank and a plank* (or whatever she or he decides to add). By the time the game really gets going, you'll all have quite a bag. The objective is to **name everything in the bag, in sequence**, or the player is out. The **winner** is the last player who names *everything* correctly.

TODAY'S

DATE: _____   OUR WEATHER IS: _____

TODAY WE ARE IN: _____

What we did today: _____

_____

_____

_____

Things I liked best: _____

_____

_____

What I saw or heard that was funny: _____

_____

_____

Some foods I ate: _____

_____

WHAT I BOUGHT TODAY

ITEM   COST

_____ $_____

_____ $_____

_____ $_____

_____ $_____

TOTAL I SPENT TODAY: $_____

DIARY

DRAW SOMETHING YOU SAW TODAY

My picture is about: _____

_____

⭐

THE STATE GAME

The leader gets to **name a state** and the others have to figure out what the last letter is of that state, and then name another state that begins with the **last letter.** For example if the leader calls, *Minnesota,* then the last letter is an **A**. So the game is to think of states that begin with A. (Hint: Alaska or Alabama, to name just two). The winner gets to name **another state**, and the game begins all over again. A variation is to play with the names of well-known countries (France, Japan, etc.) or world-famous cities (Paris, London), instead of state names.

TODAY'S

DATE: OUR WEATHER IS:

TODAY WE ARE IN:

What we did today: _____

_____

_____

_____

Things I liked best: _____

_____

_____

What I saw or heard that was funny: _____

_____

_____

Some foods I ate: _____

_____

WHAT I BOUGHT TODAY

ITEM   COST

_____ $_____

_____ $_____

_____ $_____

_____ $_____

TOTAL I SPENT TODAY: $_____

DIARY

DRAW SOMETHING YOU SAW TODAY

My picture is about: _____

_____

 TV GAME SHOW

All right, now you're on **television.** One of you is the **game-show** Moderator; the rest are guest panelists. The **moderator** picks a thing or an object (no people or ideas, please) and announces only that it's animal, mineral or vegetable. Then the **panelists** each in turn ask **one** question, such as, *"is it bigger than a cat?"* The moderator can only say, *yes or no.* The panel has only **21 questions** to use up; otherwise the game is over. Whoever wins is the next Moderator.

TODAY'S

DATE: _____ OUR WEATHER IS: _____

TODAY WE ARE IN: _____

What we did today: _____

_____

_____

_____

Things I liked best: _____

_____

_____

What I saw or heard that was funny: _____

_____

_____

Some foods I ate: _____

_____

🦋 WHAT I BOUGHT TODAY

ITEM   COST

_____ $_____

_____ $_____

_____ $_____

_____ $_____

TOTAL I SPENT TODAY: $_____

DIARY

DRAW SOMETHING YOU SAW TODAY

My picture is about: _____

_____

_____

  THE TALE TELLERS

Everyone loves a **good story,** especially if he or she doesn't know where it will end. In Tale Teller, someone **starts a story**—one that he or she makes up or one that is already known. At an exciting place, the moderator calls, *"Stop!"* Then the **next person** continues telling the story—**his or her way, and with some variations**. Sometimes, the story really gets switched around! At another exciting place, *"Stop!"* is called—then another tale teller takes over. Sometimes, the next tale teller will go on with his or her own story by saying, *"But while this was happening...."* You get the idea. The story goes on for as long as tale tellers tell tales. And **you** know how long that is.

TODAY'S

DATE: OUR WEATHER IS:

TODAY WE ARE IN:

What we did today: _____

_____

_____

_____

Things I liked best: _____

_____

_____

What I saw or heard that was funny: _____

_____

_____

Some foods I ate: _____

_____

WHAT I BOUGHT TODAY

ITEM   COST

_____ $_____

_____ $_____

_____ $_____

_____ $_____

TOTAL I SPENT TODAY: $_____

DIARY

DRAW SOMETHING YOU SAW TODAY

My picture is about: _____

_____

NAME THE TUNE

Now you get a chance to be a little **musical** (or a lot). One player names a **category** such as "blue" songs (Blue Moon, for example) or a word, and the others by turn get to **name that tune.** Some suggestions: songs that are about dances, favorite films or TV shows, travel, people's names, seasons, times of the day (such as sunset or night), or about romance. For a variation, the winner (or the loser) gets to sing them. Or everybody sings them.

TODAY'S

DATE: _____   OUR WEATHER IS: _____

TODAY WE ARE IN: _____

What we did today: _____
_____
_____
_____

Things I liked best: _____
_____
_____

What I saw or heard that was funny: _____
_____
_____

Some foods I ate: _____
_____

WHAT I BOUGHT TODAY

ITEM   COST

_____ $_____

_____ $_____

_____ $_____

_____ $_____

TOTAL I SPENT TODAY: $_____

DIARY

DRAW SOMETHING YOU SAW TODAY

My picture is about:

MINDREADERS

The moderator announces he or she has a **famous person** in mind—living or dead, but must be famous enough for everyone to recognize. The moderator says only the **first initial** of the **last name**. Then the **"mindreaders"** have to guess the name of the famous person by asking questions, beginning with, *"Are you concentrating on _____?"* The questions can only be by category, such as, *"Are you concentrating on a famous actress?" "a rock star?" "a historical figure?" "Still alive?" "A woman?"* And so on, until the famous person whose name begins with the letter is **"mindread."**

TODAY'S

DATE: _____   OUR WEATHER IS: _____

TODAY WE ARE IN: _____

What we did today: _____

_____

_____

_____

Things I liked best: _____

_____

_____

What I saw or heard that was funny: _____

_____

_____

Some foods I ate: _____

_____

WHAT I BOUGHT TODAY

ITEM	COST
_____	$_____
_____	$_____
_____	$_____
_____	$_____
TOTAL I SPENT TODAY:	$_____

DIARY

DRAW SOMETHING YOU SAW TODAY

My picture is about: _____

_____

SCRAMBLE UP

Take a blank piece of paper and on it **scramble** a word so that it is not recognizable. For example, you can scramble the word, *travel,* by changing the letters around to make it read *"velart,"* which is travel scrambled up. The game is for the rest of the players to **figure out** what the scrambled word is and put the letters in correct order on their piece of paper to identify the word. Great fun! It's only fair that the best unscrambler gets to be the next word scrambler.

TODAY'S

DATE: _____ OUR WEATHER IS: _____

TODAY WE ARE IN: _____

What we did today: _____
_____
_____
_____

Things I liked best: _____
_____
_____

What I saw or heard that was funny: _____
_____
_____

Some foods I ate: _____
_____

WHAT I BOUGHT TODAY

ITEM   COST

_____ $_____

_____ $_____

_____ $_____

_____ $_____

TOTAL I SPENT TODAY: $_____

DIARY

DRAW SOMETHING YOU SAW TODAY

My picture is about:

 CRAZY PICTURES

Take a sheet of paper and **fold it in thirds**. On the **top third**, the first player draws the head and neck of a person, animal or thing, unknown to the others. When he or she is finished, the page is folded over so that just the bottom of the picture shows. The next player draws the body on the **second third** of the page. Or course, second player should not know what the first player was drawing. The third player gets to finish the **bottom third** of the sheet by drawing the legs and the feet. Unfold the sheet—and there you have a **crazy picture!** Perhaps you can even think of a fun name for your creation.

TODAY'S

DATE: _____   OUR WEATHER IS: _____

TODAY WE ARE IN: _____

What we did today: _____
_____
_____
_____

Things I liked best: _____
_____
_____

What I saw or heard that was funny: _____
_____
_____

Some foods I ate: _____
_____

WHAT I BOUGHT TODAY

ITEM   COST

_____ $_____
_____ $_____
_____ $_____
_____ $_____

TOTAL I SPENT TODAY: $_____

DIARY

DRAW SOMETHING YOU SAW TODAY

My picture is about: _____

_____

☆ THE HANGMAN

Here's an ages-old game. The hangman thinks of a word, then on a sheet of paper, draws a **dash** for **each letter** of the word, then also draws a **gallows**. The player has to guess what the word is, one letter at a time. When the letter is correct, it is drawn over the **dash;** when the player guesses wrong, the hangman draws in a **figure** on the **gallows:** first a head, then nose, mouth, eyes, ears, hair, body, hands, legs, and feet. In all, a player can get hung in **10 bad** guesses. The last thing to be drawn, of course, is the **noose.** Words to be guessed can range from simple, short words to more complex titles of songs.

TODAY'S

DATE: _____   OUR WEATHER IS: _____

TODAY WE ARE IN: _____

What we did today: _____
_____
_____
_____

Things I liked best: _____
_____
_____

What I saw or heard that was funny: _____
_____
_____

Some foods I ate: _____
_____

WHAT I BOUGHT TODAY

ITEM   COST

_____ $_____

_____ $_____

_____ $_____

_____ $_____

TOTAL I SPENT TODAY: $_____

DIARY

DRAW SOMETHING YOU SAW TODAY

My picture is about: _____

_____

 I SPY!

All the players become **"spies"** on the lookout for **something** they **agree upon** in advance. That can be most anything; for example, if the game players are in a car, that can be a red barn. Everyone tries to locate a red barn; the first to see one cries, *"I spy!"* He or she gets one point; if two say "I spy" at the same time, each get one point. Whoever gets to 10 points first **wins** and gets to pick the next object. Objects can be a bridge, a red car, a yellow sign, a horse, or even a car with a certain license plate, such as a Texas plate.

TODAY'S

DATE: _____   OUR WEATHER IS: _____

TODAY WE ARE IN: _____

What we did today: _____
_____
_____
_____

Things I liked best: _____
_____
_____

What I saw or heard that was funny: _____
_____
_____

Some foods I ate: _____
_____

WHAT I BOUGHT TODAY

ITEM	COST
_____	$_____
_____	$_____
_____	$_____
_____	$_____
TOTAL I SPENT TODAY:	$_____

DIARY

DRAW SOMETHING YOU SAW TODAY

My picture is about:

_____

_____

SIGNS O THE TIMES

Look for **signs** as you drive along and try to get **words** you see beginning with **alphabetical letters in order**. The first person to see an "A" on a word on a sign calls out *"A";* then the next person tries to find a word beginning with a "B," and so on. Letters must be in **order.** The person who sees the **most letters** from A to Z wins. But be warned: You'll really have to look hard for some letters, like *X and Z.*

TODAY'S

DATE: _____   OUR WEATHER IS: _____

TODAY WE ARE IN: _____

What we did today: _____

_____

_____

_____

Things I liked best: _____

_____

_____

What I saw or heard that was funny: _____

_____

_____

Some foods I ate: _____

_____

WHAT I BOUGHT TODAY

ITEM   COST

_____ $ _____

_____ $ _____

_____ $ _____

_____ $ _____

TOTAL I SPENT TODAY: $ _____

DIARY

DRAW SOMETHING YOU SAW TODAY

My picture is about: _____

_____

_____

FAMOUS ME

Here's everybody's chance to be a **star** or a **celebrity**. One person is **Famous Me**—a person **well known** in history, television, motion pictures or sports. The players ask the "celebrity" questions to find out his or her identity, but the famous person can only answer with a *yes* or a *no*. (Or a nod or shake of the head). The limit is 16 questions. Whoever guesses right can be the **famous person next**.

TODAY'S

DATE: _____   OUR WEATHER IS: _____

TODAY WE ARE IN: _____

What we did today: _____
_____
_____
_____

Things I liked best: _____
_____
_____

What I saw or heard that was funny: _____
_____
_____

Some foods I ate: _____
_____

WHAT I BOUGHT TODAY

ITEM	COST
_____	$_____
_____	$_____
_____	$_____
_____	$_____
TOTAL I SPENT TODAY:	$_____

DIARY

DRAW SOMETHING YOU SAW TODAY

My picture is about: _____

_____

_____

WHAT'S HAPPENING?

One person carefully acts out an **every day deed**—in pantomime. For example, the person may be watching a ping pong game (with head going back and forth) or brushing teeth or even driving a car. The players each take turns guessing what's happening. The winner gets to be the next one to perform a pantomime.

TODAY'S

DATE: _____ OUR WEATHER IS: _____

TODAY WE ARE IN: _____

What we did today: _____

_____

_____

_____

Things I liked best: _____

_____

_____

What I saw or heard that was funny: _____

_____

_____

Some foods I ate: _____

_____

WHAT I BOUGHT TODAY

ITEM   COST

_____ $_____

_____ $_____

_____ $_____

_____ $_____

TOTAL I SPENT TODAY: $_____

DIARY

DRAW SOMETHING YOU SAW TODAY

My picture is about: _____

_____

_____

RAPPING WITH RHYMES

Here's your chance to do some mini **"raps"** with words you see along the way, such as on billboard or other signs. For example, if you see a sign that says, "Stop Ahead," you can use it in a **rhyming rap** that goes, *"If you don't...Stop Ahead—You can get...a bop on the head."* Everybody can take turns, or players can be chosen to **rap with signs** that everyone sees. *(And if you don't...see any signs—you're just not going to have...any good times.)*

TODAY'S

DATE: OUR WEATHER IS:

TODAY WE ARE IN:

What we did today: _____
_____
_____
_____

Things I liked best: _____

_____

_____

What I saw or heard that was funny: _____

_____

_____

Some foods I ate: _____

_____

WHAT I BOUGHT TODAY

ITEM   COST

_____ $_____

_____ $_____

_____ $_____

_____ $_____

TOTAL I SPENT TODAY: $_____

DIARY

DRAW SOMETHING YOU SAW TODAY

My picture is about: _____

_____

_____

OPPOSITES

They say **opposites attract,** and in fact, one opposite will attract another in this game. Choose up sides so each person has an "opponent." In turn, each opponent says **one word,** and his or her opponent says **the opposite of the word** previously said. For example, one says *no,* the other *yes; stormy, fair skies,* and so on. Here's the catch: each has only **three seconds** to answer. The player giving the most answers in a certain time wins, or goes on to play other winners in a group.

TODAY'S

DATE: _____ OUR WEATHER IS: _____

TODAY WE ARE IN: _____

What we did today: _____

_____

_____

_____

Things I liked best: _____

_____

_____

What I saw or heard that was funny: _____

_____

_____

Some foods I ate: _____

_____

WHAT I BOUGHT TODAY

ITEM	COST
_____	$_____
_____	$_____
_____	$_____
_____	$_____

TOTAL I SPENT TODAY: $_____

DIARY

DRAW SOMETHING YOU SAW TODAY

My picture is about: _____

_____

_____

EEK! HOW AWFUL

Into a **paper bag**, secretly collect a few items such as a grape, a sock, a feather, a paper clip, a coin—the more fun the better. Players in turn close their eyes, then **insert their hand** to feel and touch the objects and to **describe them**. *Eek! How Awful.* You'll be surprised how *imaginative* the answers you can get from ordinary, everyday things.

TODAY'S

DATE: _____   OUR WEATHER IS: _____

TODAY WE ARE IN: _____

What we did today: _____

_____

_____

_____

Things I liked best: _____

_____

_____

What I saw or heard that was funny: _____

_____

_____

Some foods I ate: _____

_____

WHAT I BOUGHT TODAY

ITEM	COST
_____	$ _____
_____	$ _____
_____	$ _____
_____	$ _____
TOTAL I SPENT TODAY:	$ _____

DIARY

DRAW SOMETHING YOU SAW TODAY

My picture is about:

⭐ ⭐ FOLLOW ME

Everyone **follows** the leader's activity – then **adds one activity** of his or her own. For example, the game can be started by the leader holding his or her nose. The next person has to follow this example by holding his or her nose then adding **one more** activity, such as sneezing. The next person, in turn, holds his or her nose, sneezes, then adds something new (like snapping fingers). The game goes on with each player adding **one more thing** after **exactly repeating** what went on before. The player who misses a thing is out. The winner is the player who correctly repeats everything the longest.

TODAY'S

DATE: OUR WEATHER IS:

TODAY WE ARE IN:

What we did today: _____

_____

_____

_____

Things I liked best: _____

_____

_____

What I saw or heard that was funny: _____

_____

_____

Some foods I ate: _____

_____

WHAT I BOUGHT TODAY

ITEM   COST

_____ $_____

_____ $_____

_____ $_____

_____ $_____

TOTAL I SPENT TODAY: $_____

DIARY

DRAW SOMETHING YOU SAW TODAY

My picture is about: _____

_____

_____

CHARADES

One person will make up a **charade**, and the rest will try to **guess.** The subject can be the name of a TV show, a movie, book, or a song title. The player holds up his or her fingers to indicate **number** of words. Then, he or she holds up a finger to indicate **first word,** second word, so on, while performing a charade. Everyone tries to guess what's going on—and the winner is the person who correctly guesses the full name or title. **A variation:** Instead of acting them out, the leader draws **pictures** for each word.

Who Me?

TODAY'S

DATE: OUR WEATHER IS:

TODAY WE ARE IN:

What we did today: _____
_____
_____
_____

Things I liked best: _____
_____
_____

What I saw or heard that was funny: _____
_____
_____

Some foods I ate: _____
_____

WHAT I BOUGHT TODAY

ITEM	COST
_____	$_____
_____	$_____
_____	$_____
_____	$_____
TOTAL I SPENT TODAY:	$_____

DIARY

DRAW SOMETHING YOU SAW TODAY

My picture is about:

_____

_____

HOTTER—COLDER

Here the main player decides on an **object** within the car or room, and everyone tries to **learn what it is**. The main player will say *hotter* when the guesses are in the right direction; *colder* when they are going the wrong way. Winner gets to be the main player.

♥·♥·♥ TODAY'S

DATE: OUR WEATHER IS:

TODAY WE ARE IN:

What we did today: _____

_____

_____

_____

Things I liked best: _____

_____

_____

What I saw or heard that was funny: _____

_____

_____

Some foods I ate: _____

_____

WHAT I BOUGHT TODAY

ITEM	COST
_____	$_____
_____	$_____
_____	$_____
_____	$_____

TOTAL I SPENT TODAY: $_____

DIARY

DRAW SOMETHING YOU SAW TODAY

My picture is about: _____

_____

 THE AWFUL CAT

Here's a word game to see how many, and often ridiculous ways, you can **describe that Awful Cat**. Beginning with the **A** letter, the first person says, "The neighbor's cat is an *awful* cat." The next person repeats, but has to think up another way to describe the cat, beginning with the **letter A,** such as *atrocious, athletic, arty*, or even *artificial* cat. When a round has been completed, go on to the **next letter** of the alphabet, B, (*bedeviled, bald,* etc) and so on. If the player doesn't think of a word within **15 seconds**, she or he can only **yowl or meow** when his or her turn comes next. Winner is the last one remaining to describe that awful cat.

TODAY'S

DATE: OUR WEATHER IS:

TODAY WE ARE IN:

What we did today: _____

_____

_____

_____

Things I liked best: _____

_____

_____

What I saw or heard that was funny: _____

_____

_____

Some foods I ate: _____

_____

WHAT I BOUGHT TODAY

ITEM	COST
_____	$_____
_____	$_____
_____	$_____
_____	$_____
TOTAL I SPENT TODAY:	$_____

DIARY

DRAW SOMETHING YOU SAW TODAY

My picture is about: _____

_____

SIMON SAYS

Here's a fun game that's a lot more complicated than it sounds. One player is "Simon," and only he or she **gives the orders.** The object of the game is to only follow those orders specifically **preceded** by the words, *"Simon Says."* For example, if Simon says, *"sit up!"* and a person sits up, then that person is **out** of the game. However, if *Simon says: "Simon says, 'sit up,'"* that's a **correct** order. Once Simon starts giving orders quickly, then one by one players will drop out. Some examples of orders: *Hold out your hands...hands up! Simon says, hands up. Turn around...look right.* Of course, Simon has to say it **first** for it to be a proper command. Winner gets to be Simon.

TODAY'S

DATE: _____   OUR WEATHER IS: _____

TODAY WE ARE IN: _____

What we did today: _____
_____
_____
_____

Things I liked best: _____
_____
_____

What I saw or heard that was funny: _____
_____
_____

Some foods I ate: _____
_____

WHAT I BOUGHT TODAY

ITEM   COST

_____ $_____
_____ $_____
_____ $_____
_____ $_____

TOTAL I SPENT TODAY: $_____

DIARY

DRAW SOMETHING YOU SAW TODAY

My picture is about:

_____

_____

_____

MIRROR IMAGE

One person is chosen to be the **mirror,** and the rest of the players **mirror him or her** for two minutes. The idea is that each player must be an **exact mirror image of the mirror**—often with funny results (some people are cracked mirrors). Here are some basic things the group might try to mirror image: stick out a tongue, laugh heartily, cross eyes, wink one eye at a time, meow piteously, pretend to drive a car, fly an airplane, or sail a boat.

TODAY'S

DATE: _____ OUR WEATHER IS: _____

TODAY WE ARE IN: _____

What we did today: _____
_____
_____
_____

Things I liked best: _____
_____
_____

What I saw or heard that was funny: _____
_____
_____

Some foods I ate: _____
_____

WHAT I BOUGHT TODAY

ITEM   COST

_____ $_____

_____ $_____

_____ $_____

_____ $_____

TOTAL I SPENT TODAY: $_____

DIARY

DRAW SOMETHING YOU SAW TODAY

My picture is about: _____

_____

_____

JOLLY GREEN GIANT

As we all know, the Jolly Green Giant goes **"ho, ho."** In this game, the first player says, "ho." The second player says, "ho, ho." And so on around the ring of players, each adding a ho-hoing in his or her own way, **in the right number,** and each adding a ho! With a little imagination, the ho-hoing can be hilarious. Anyone can laugh—except the person ho-hoing. That person must not laugh while ho-hoing or else be eliminated from the game. The one who has the most staying power, and **remembers the right number of ho-hoes**, is the winner.

TODAY'S

DATE: _____   OUR WEATHER IS: _____

TODAY WE ARE IN: _____

What we did today: _____
_____
_____
_____

Things I liked best: _____
_____
_____

What I saw or heard that was funny: _____
_____
_____

Some foods I ate: _____
_____

WHAT I BOUGHT TODAY

ITEM	COST
_____	$_____
_____	$_____
_____	$_____
_____	$_____
TOTAL I SPENT TODAY:	$_____

DIARY

DRAW SOMETHING YOU SAW TODAY

My picture is about: _____

_____

_____

CONTACT!

While you're in the family car, traveling along, try this game of coordination. The idea here is for the players (except for the driver, of course!) to **choose an object** that you can see **not too far ahead,** such as a historical marker, a famous landmark, or even a car in the opposite lane. All players close their eyes, and when each thinks the chosen object is exactly alongside, he or she hollers, *"contact,"* then opens his or her eyes. Winner is the person who guesses correctly or is closest. An alternative to this group game is for each player *in turn* to play **contact.**

❤ ˙ ❤ ˙ ❤ ˙ ❤ TODAY'S

DATE: OUR WEATHER IS:

TODAY WE ARE IN:

What we did today: _____

_____

_____

_____

Things I liked best: _____

_____

_____

What I saw or heard that was funny: _____

_____

_____

Some foods I ate: _____

_____

WHAT I BOUGHT TODAY

ITEM   COST

_____ $_____

_____ $_____

_____ $_____

_____ $_____

❤   ❤   ❤   TOTAL I SPENT TODAY: $_____

DIARY ♥ ♥ ♥ ♥ ♥

DRAW SOMETHING YOU SAW TODAY

My picture is about: _____

_____

_____

♥ ♥ **DUPLICATING MACHINES**

One person is chosen as **It**, who begins the game by making some **motion,** such as rubbing his or her nose. Then It points to another player, who, in turn, has to **duplicate** what It has done and **add one more motion** of his or her own. This player, in turn, points to another player who has to duplicate all that has gone on before—plus **add one more.** All motions have to be in proper sequence. Winner is the person who duplicates all motions without getting anything out of sequence.

EXTRA GAMES TO PLAY

Going on a Sailing Trip

You're going **sailing** for a long time and you have to take things along with you. Trouble is, you can only take along things beginning with the letter *S*. So can your crew. You begin by saying, *"I'm going on a sailing trip and I'm taking along a **snake**."* Your other players also have to **repeat** what you said, then **add one thing** of their own. This also must begin with an **S**. Those who forget the sequence, or can't think of something to take along beginning with an S, are out. Winner is the last person still going. (Then, you can start the game all over again with a *new* letter).

 Tic Tac Toe

On a piece of paper, draw **two lines** *up* and down and two lines *sideways*. Each player in turn gets to place a **mark** of an X or an O in each small square. The player that first gets **three marks** in row wins. Rows must be vertical, diagonal or horizonal lines. Like this:

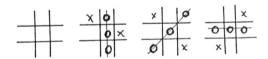

You can play a **variation** by making the same four lines, but then *closing* the ends into a **box.** Instead of playing the boxes, you play your X and O's where the lines meet (on the **intersections**.) Take a look at the illustration below. Get the idea? You need three in a **row** to win.

Alphabet Game

As you go down the road, or look around a place, you can play the Alphabet Game. Look for **signs** that have **letters.** Begin looking for the letter **A.** The **first person** to see an A gets 1 point. Write what you saw down (and the initials of who saw it) Then look for the letter **B** and so on. You need to go in alphabetical order. The **first person** to name the letter gets the point. The player with the most points wins.

A/_____   N_____
B/_____   O_____
C/_____   P_____
D/_____   Q_____
E/_____   R_____
F/_____   S_____
G/_____   T_____
H/_____   U_____
I/_____   V_____
J/_____   W_____
K/_____   X_____
L/_____   Y_____
M/_____   Z_____

Popeye

This is a game kids can play at **night.** Look for a car with just **one headlight,** the *"Popeye."* The first person to see this yells, *"Popeye,"* and gets to touch, slap or punch the person next to him or her on the shoulder. Agree on what you are going to do in advance, but be careful not hit too hard, please!)

The Color Purple

The main player **picks something** inside the car, train or plane (however you're traveling) which is a certain **color**, such as *purple*. He or she then says, *"Color me purple,"* and in turn, others try to guess **what object** he or she has chosen. If a couple of rounds don't locate the specific item, then players can ask specific questions as to its **size** or **location**. Winner gets to pick the next color and object.

 Blind artist

Get a sheet of paper and a pencil. **Blindfold** whoever is "it," and then place the tip of the pencil on the paper. The blindfolded person is then told what to **draw**—an airplane, a car or a ship. The fun comes as everyone sees what the blind artist tries to draw. Take turns.

Cross the Creek

Here's a game for inside your motel or hotel room. Get some pieces of **paper** (maybe a newspaper) and one person lays pieces in an **irregular line**, but stepping distance apart. These are **stepping stones**. Each person has to step carefully or he or she will end up in the creek. The rules are that only **ONE FOOT** can be on a "stone" at a time. For an added variation after a couple of games, certain really smart persons can also **balance a book** on their heads. If they step off the "stone" or lose their book, they fall in the creek—and are out.

It's a goal!

In your hotel or motel room, a **wastebasket** can become a basketball **hoop.** Sheets of paper are wadded up into **"balls,"** or socks are rolled together into balls and each player gets a toss. As everyone gets better at the game, the basket can be moved farther away. First one to get to **21 points** wins. After a while, you can also place the "goal" against a wall for a bank shot, or prop it at an angle against a chair.

Two games with pennies

Lucky Pennies

First game:

You will need **10 pennies** per player. Taking turns, each player secretly puts a number of **pennies** in his or her **closed hand.** The object of the game is to take turns **guessing** how many **pennies** the player has in hand. *Winner gets the pennies.* But if the guessers do not name the correct amount in the hand, they **lose** from their penny hoard the amount the player **had in hand. Hint:** Play with just a few pennies at first.

Second game:

Odd or even?

A longer-lasting variation: You can play this game with just one opponent. The player again **secretly** places from **one to ten pennies** in his or her closed hand, then places the hand in front of the opponent. The opponent must guess **odd** or **even** amounts of pennies. If he or she is right, the opponent wins a penny. If he or she is incorrect, the opponent loses a penny. The game goes on until no pennies are left to play with, or, after a certain amount of time has gone by, the winner is the one with the most pennies.

***Note:** You can also play this game with toothpicks, marbles, or other small objects.

What are these pictures trying to tell us?

The answer is at bottom of the page

Charade Pictures

You play this game by **drawing pictures,** instead of **acting out** a charade. The first player chooses a **topic,** as in charades. She or he can choose from a title of a popular kid's book, a well-known song, or a hit movie. Also, the player can choose a funny or contemporary saying, or the title or something from a famous nursery rhyme. The fun part is that he or she can't use any words.

On a piece of paper, he or she **draws** pictures representing the charade on paper. The opposing players try to guess the subject. The person who guesses the topic the quickest is the winner and gets one point. Then, it's time to change, and the winner has a turn to be the main player.

You also can divide into teams, if you like, and decide jointly how you want to present your subject.

 ————————————————————

ANSWER: The boy at left has his hands up by ears, as if they were large, and is gently making a mooing noise. He is trying to represent a cow. In the center picture, the boy is jumping up (see his feet?). In the last picture, we see a moon. What is the Picture Charade? If you guessed, *The Cow Jumped Over the Moon,* you were 100 percent right.

Guess the Charade Picture

Here are some **charade pictures** for you to guess (or to use in your games). The answers are at the bottom of the page.

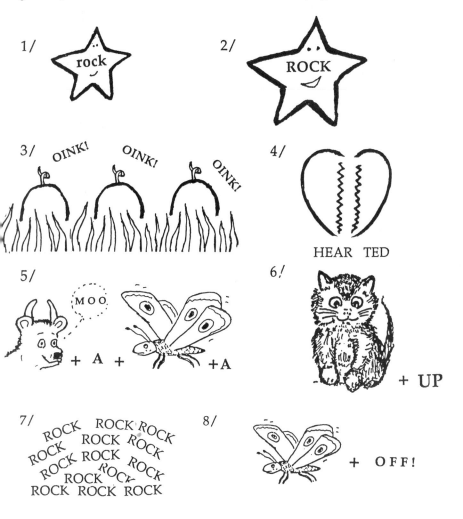

1/

2/

3/   OINK!   OINK!   OINK!

4/

HEAR   TED

5/   MOO

+ A +   +A

6/

+ UP

7/   ROCK ROCK ROCK
ROCK ROCK ROCK
ROCK ROCK ROCK
ROCK ROCK ROCK
ROCK ROCK
ROCK ROCK ROCK

8/

+ OFF!

Charade Picture Answers: 1/ Rock star 2/ **Big rock star** 3/ Three Little Pigs (tails-up in tall grass) 4/ Broken hearted 5/ Cowabunga (a saying) 6/ Catsup 7/ A pile of rocks or a rock pile 8/ Bug off (as in, "get out of here!")

Fencing Kids

It's sort of like a **mini-fencing match** in which you and your opponent can make **thrusts** with your trusty pencil. You can fence **sideways,** and **up and down,** *between the dots.* You **can't** move **diagonally.** Each player gets **one move** at a time to **connect two dots.** Then, it's the other player's turn. Your goal is to complete a **square** to put your **initial in it.** Then you get **another turn.** If you see someone else closing a square, you can **block their move** by putting in your line when your turn comes. And, of course, you have to be careful not to get caught connecting the **third side** of a box when your turn comes, because then your opponent then can close the box to claim the point. The champion kid fencer is the one with the most squares. Game hint: different colored pencils help keep track of each player. Or one player can use a line and another a series of dashes.

Round 1/   Round 2/

.   .   .   .

.   .   .   .

.   .   .   .

.   .   .   .

.   .   .   .

Round 3/ Round 4/

Round 5/ Round 6/

Round 7/ Round 8/

Round 9/   Round 10/

Round 11/   Round 12/

Round 13/   Round 14/

Round 15/

Round 16/

Round 17/

Round 18/

Round 19/

Round 20/

 **Circle Games**

Try to find the **words** spelled out below. Each circle contains just **one** word. Your job is to figure out the word. You must find the **starting letter** and then read **clockwise** (the way a clock turns). You can't skip a letter. For example, in the circle game *above*, the starting letter is *C*. Reading clockwise, you will find that the word is *"CAR."* (Don't peek now, but the answers are on the bottom of the page, upside down)

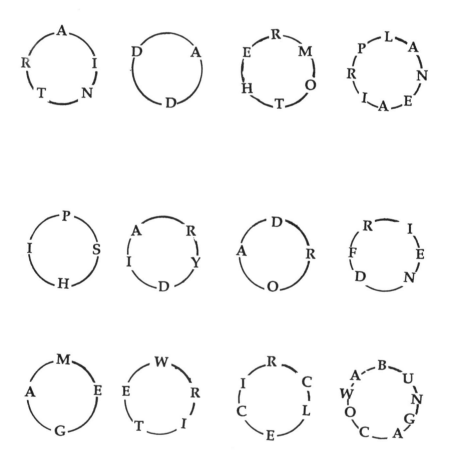

Answers: Train, dad, mother, airplane, ship, diary, road, friend, game, write, circle, cowabunga

WORD GAMES

Rapid Riddles

1/ What do you have that others use more than you when you travel?

2/ What smells the most in the car?

3/ It falls down all the time, but never gets hurt. What is it?

4/ You give this away all the time, but still you can keep it. What is it?

5/ What kind of coat can you put on wet and still be happy with?

6/ What is black and white. but red all over?

7/ What's very light but you can't hold for long?

8/ What is faster—hot or cold?

9/ What word do you always pronounce wrong?

10/ Even when the world seems dark and gloomy, where can you always find happiness?

Silly States—Do You Live in Nooger?

Oh, my! Someone has misspelled the following states—and you have to be a detective and put them back in order. For example, "Sotaminne," isn't a soft drink. It's the state of Minnesota, all scrambled up. Here are some more states for you to unscramble:

1/ Sinconwis
2/ Sexta
3/ Enw orky
4/ Ouths Kotada
5/ Nooger
6/ Ippssimissm
7/ Driflao
8/ Sillioni
9/ Enaim
10/ Doahi

Silly States Answers: 1/ Wisconsin 2/ Texas 3/ New York 4/South Dakota 5/ Oregon 6/ Mississippi 7/ Florida 8/Illinois 9/ Maine 10/ Idaho

Rapid Riddles Answers: 1/Your name 2/Your nose 3/ Rain 4/ Your word 5/ Coat of paint 6/ A newspaper (red is read) 7/ Your breath 8/ Hot, because you can catch cold 9/ The word, wrong 10/ In your dictionary.

CAR GAMES

Try to **identify** each of the following. Write your **initials** if you are the **first** to see each item. The winner is the one who has seen the **most** subjects the first.

_____Car with open trunk
_____Car with hood up
_____Car with trailer hitch
_____Car with door open
_____Car the same kind and color as your own
_____Car with spare tire carried on rear end
_____Convertible car (with or without top down)
_____Station Wagon
_____Volkswagen "beetle"
_____Car with luggage on top

Colorfully yours

Try to find things that are of the following **colors**. The **first** to see these writes it down, and, puts his or her **initials** after each, to indicate he or she is the one who saw it first:

1/ White

2/ Black

3/ Blue

4/ Red

5/ Yellow

6/ Green

7/ Orange

8/ Pink

PART THREE

MEMORIES

MY FINAL THOUGHTS
ABOUT THIS TRIP

THINGS I SAVED FROM MY TRIP

NAMES, ADDRESSES & PLACES
TO REMEMBER

MY FINAL THOUGHTS ABOUT THIS TRIP

Did you have a good time? What good times did you especially **like**. Did you have some "worst moments?" (Hint: *every* trip has these). Would you change anything the next time you travel? Lastly, you can "rate" your trip on a scale of 1 to 10. Make 10 the very best; 1 the worst ever. Be honest now.

My final comments: _____

_____

_____

I especially remember these good times: _____

_____

_____

_____

My worst moments: _____

_____

_____

What I'd do differently the next time I travel: _____

_____

_____

On a scale of 1 (worst) to 10 (best), I'd rate this trip:_____

MEMORIES

Things I saved from my trip

In **Memories** you can keep small personal **mementoes** of your vacation. Some souvenirs you might want to keep are **ticket stubs** to a favorite place or fun ride, a picture **postcard** that you picked out, **printed materials** you saved from places you visited, some foreign **currency** samples, if you went abroad, or even a favorite **photograph.** Under each item write a **few words** that will help you remember, such as the date, where you were, what it was like, or where you got the item. Be creative.

 MORE MEMORIES FROM MY TRIP

MORE MEMORIES FROM MY TRIP

NAMES, ADDRESSES & PLACES TO REMEMBER

Travel is an adventure. You will be making new friends as you travel as well as seeing interesting places. Here you can write down names and addresses, so that later you can keep in touch with them.

Name

Address

City   State   Zip

Age   Phone   E-mail

Name

Address

City   State   Zip

Age   Phone   E-mail

Name

Address

City   State   Zip

Age   Phone   E-mail

Name

Address

City   State   Zip

Age   Phone   E-mail